Somethi
beginnin
with...

INTRODUCTION

Whether you are sitting on a bus, picnicking in a park or just stuck in the house on a rainy day, everyone has played i-SPY at some time or another. The delight of spying things yourself and ticking off your score, or making your friends and family guess at your own i-SPIES, never fails to amuse.

So get out and explore all around you to get those valuable i-SPY points. Unlike other i-SPY books you no longer have to restrict yourself to car journeys or train journeys, visits to the seaside or looking out for cars. Almost anywhere you find yourself or whatever you are doing, there will be things to spot in this book. Some of them will be very easy to find and will crop up in many real world locations while others may involve trips to zoos, parks, farms or even school!

There is a later section in the book for those who like to play traditional i-SPY with their friends and family shouting out a letter and making them guess what you have seen. You can use it to get inspiration if you are stuck for finding something to make people guess, or you might use it to help you guess what someone else is asking you to spot. Or if like some people, you play your i-SPY by going through the alphabet finding something for every letter, it might help you find something for those tricky letters at the end of the alphabet!

However you play your i-SPY you will be sure to find i-SPY Something beginning with... to be a lot of fun. So get out and get spying and once you have earned 1,000 points you can claim your i-SPY badge and certificate.

How to use your i-SPY book

The items in this book are arranged alphabetically with two pages for each letter. Points values in circles or stars are shown alongside a picture of the thing you need to find, with stars representing harder to spot items. You need 1000 points to send off for your i-SPY certificate (see page 64) but that is not too difficult because there are masses of points in every book. As you make each i-SPY, write your score in the circle or star. The main book only shows a selection of things that you could find. At the back of the book there is a section where you can record any other interesting things you see while playing i-SPY.

Top 40 Spot!

apple
5
aeroplane
10
artist
alarm
clock
30
20
10
Afghan
hound
angler
20
15
abacus

ant
ammonite fossil
athlete
Top Spot!
anchor
Top Spot!
AMBULANCE
AMBULANCE
YX57 HKW
ambulance
aubergine
ape

5
belt
Top 50 Spot!
badger
builder
bowling ball
20
20
10
bike
bench
15
blackbird

boxing glove
bananas
banjo
balloon
lueberries
Waterloo 211
abellio
bus
breakdancer
Top Spot!

20
chicken
cyclist
10
crane
20
cat
5
10
cauliflower
candlestick
15
carriage
Top
40
Spot

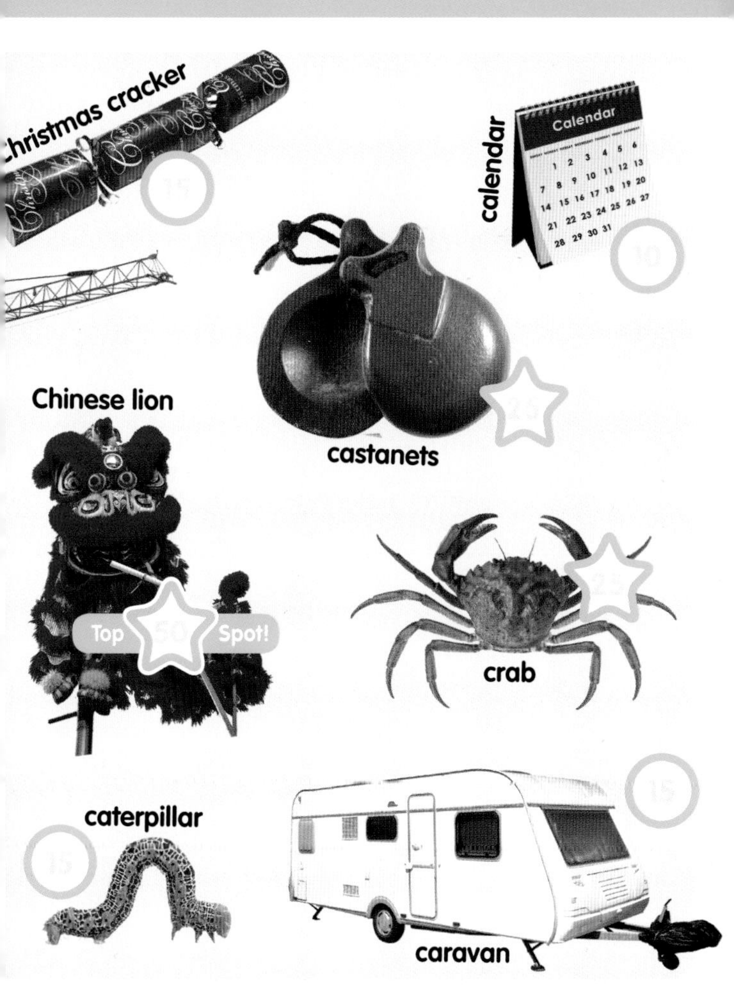
Christmas cracker
calendar
Calendar
castanets
Chinese lion
Top
Spot!
crab
caterpillar
caravan

dice
5
dachshund
20
donkey
25
dandelion
10
doctor
15
diamond
15
Danish pastry
10

drill
DVD
dolphin
dartboard
door knocker
Top Spot!
dove
drone
Top Spot!

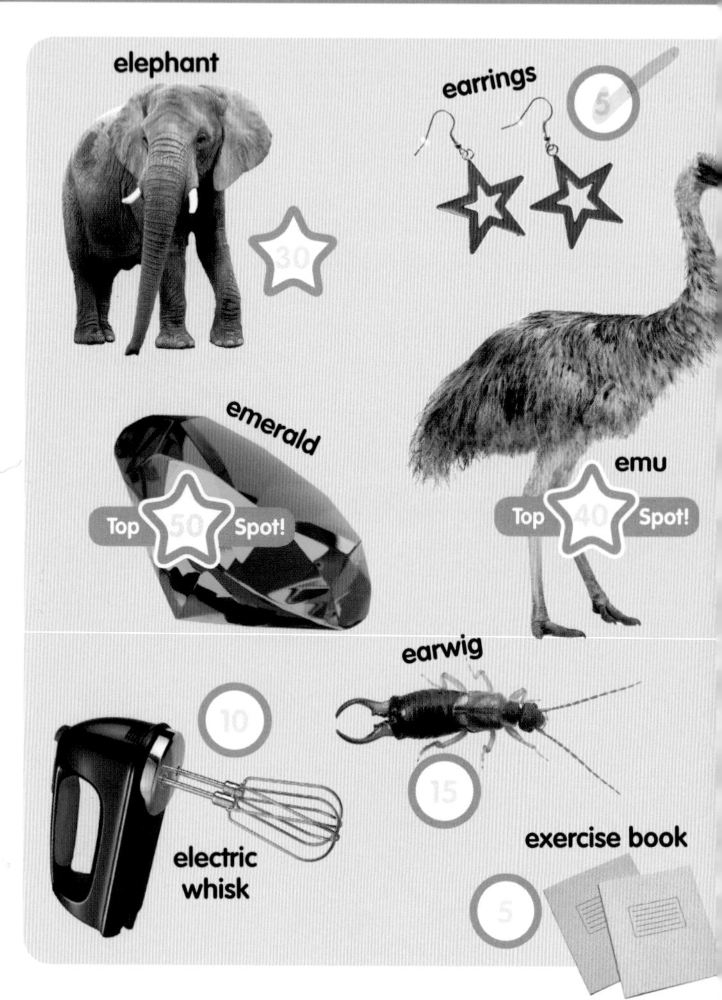
elephant
30
earrings
5
emerald
Top 50 Spot!
emu
Top 40 Spot!
earwig
10
15
electric whisk
exercise book
5

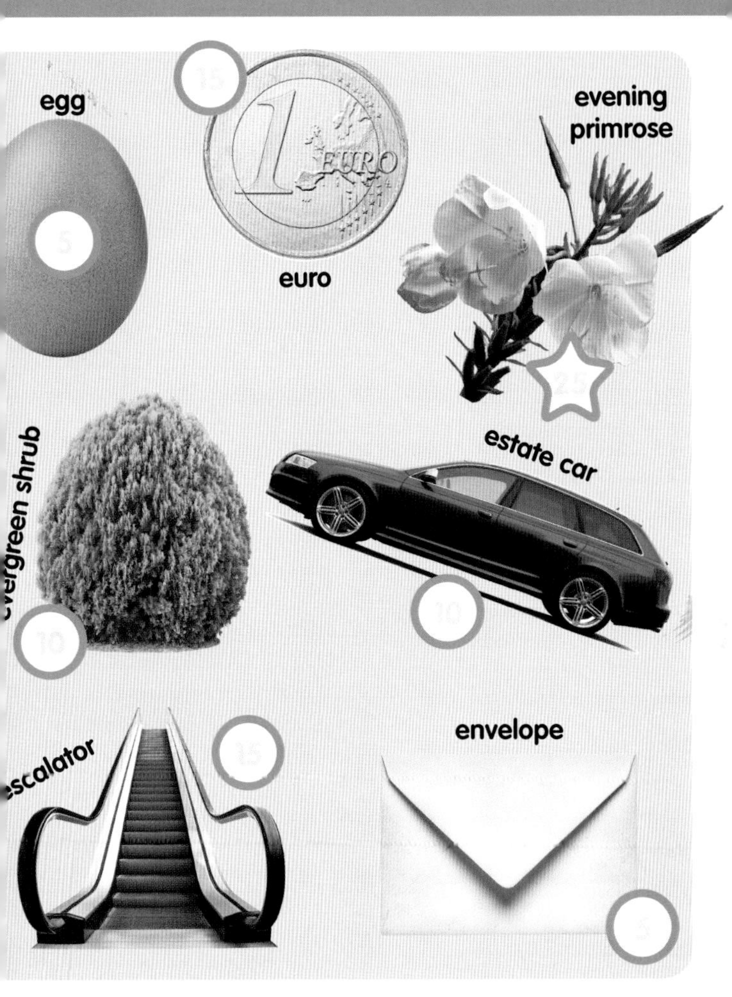
egg
euro
evening primrose
evergreen shrub
estate car
escalator
envelope

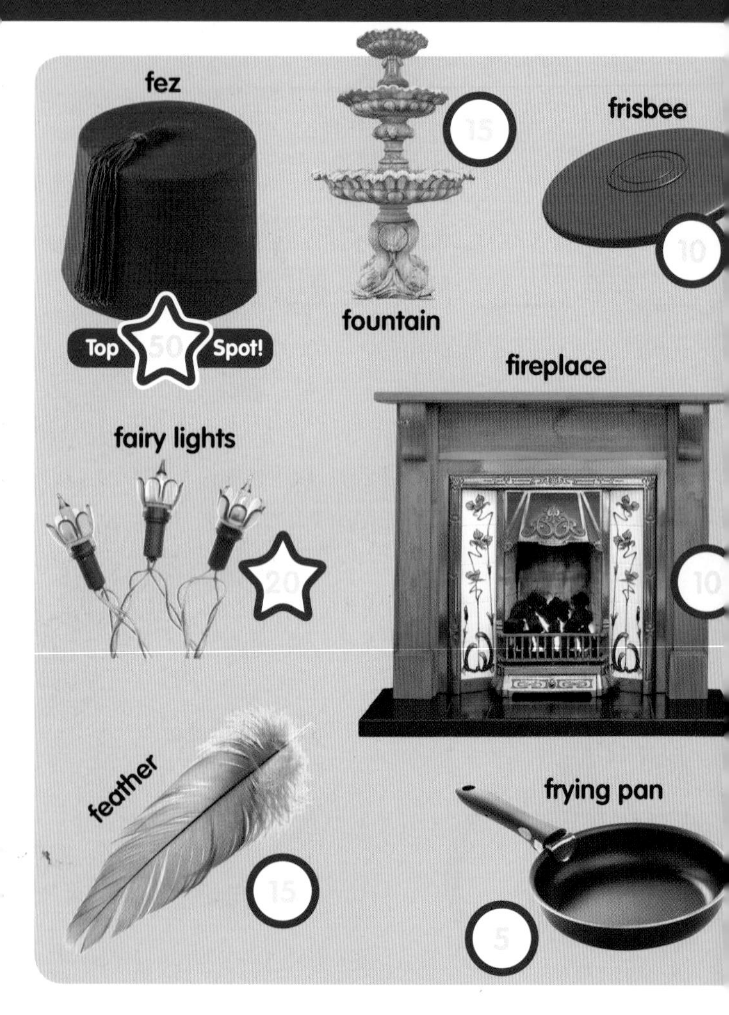
fez
Top 50 Spot!
fountain
15
frisbee
10
fireplace
10
fairy lights
20
feather
15
frying pan
5

fox
Top Spot!
footbridge
fax machine
foxglove
fancy dress
fence
fountain pen

goat
25
gate
10
glitt
bal
10
25
glasses
case
gloves
5
golf club
goldfish
15
20

grain silo
grapes
gravel
Top
Spot!
gardener
gravy boat
grand piano
garlic
Top
Spot!

hammer
15
hazelnut
5
handkerchief
10
hawthorn
15
headphones
10
honeycomb
Top 40 Spot!
hot-air balloon
25

heron
holly
horse
hedgehog
helicopter
hot-water bottle
harp
Top Spot!

ironing board
5
inflatable ball
10
icicles
Top
Sp
50
iceberg lettu
5
10
ice-cream van
Ice Cream
Wall's
Solero
ivy
15
ice skater
25

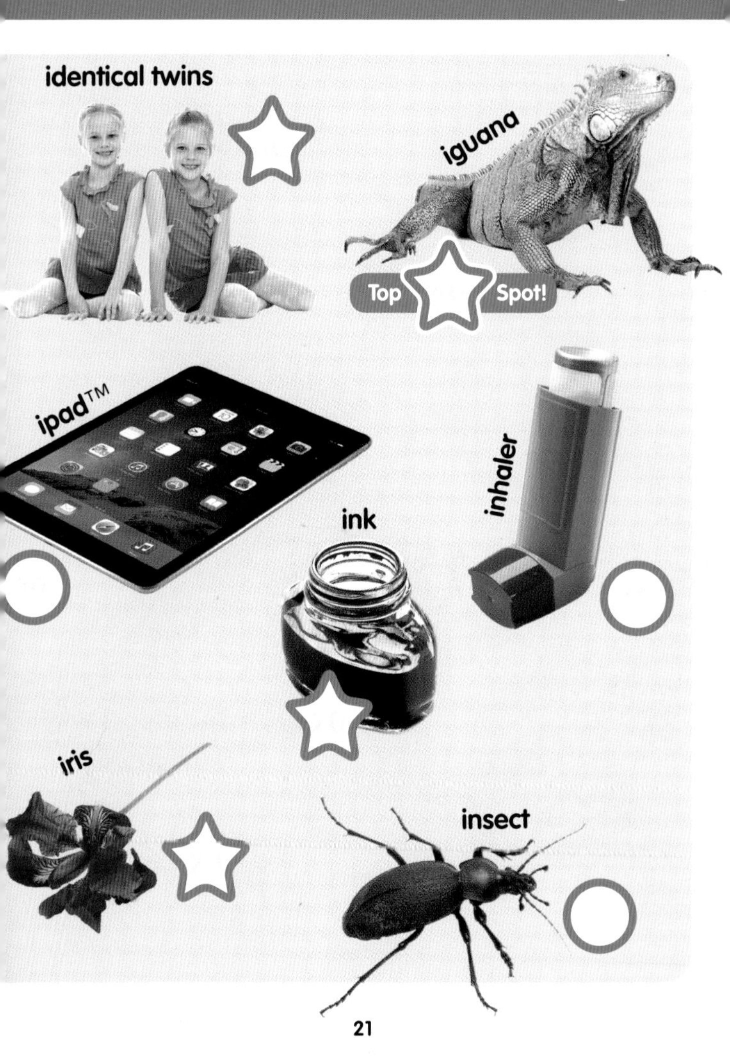
identical twins
iguana
Top
Spot!
ipad™
inhaler
ink
iris
insect

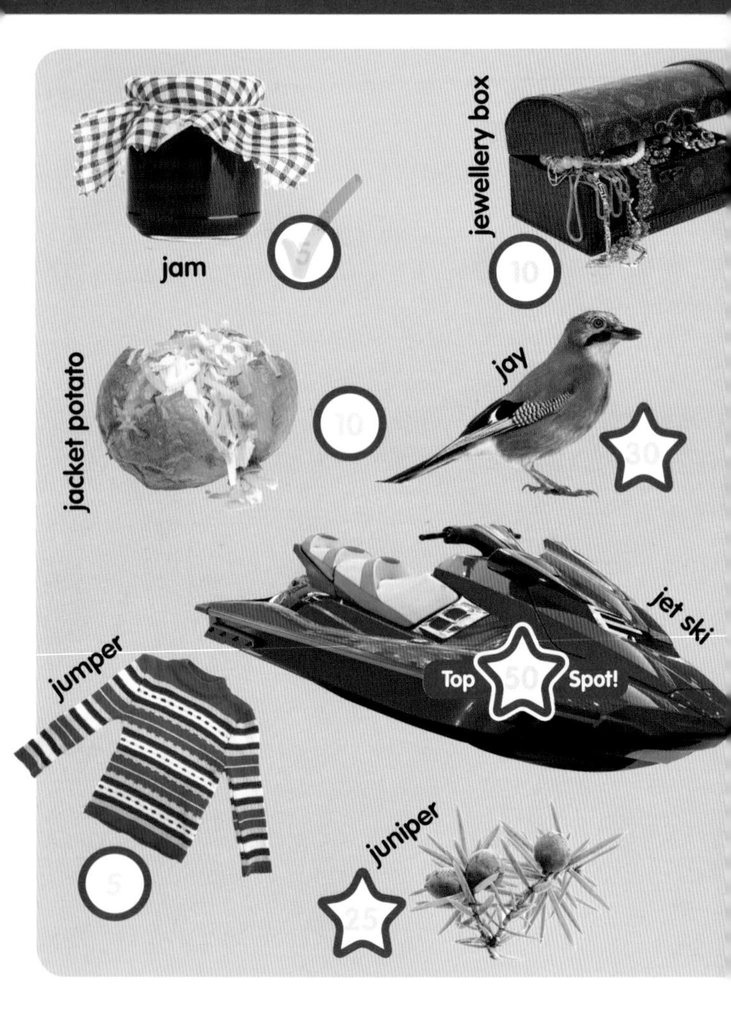
jam
jewellery box
10
jacket potato
10
jay
30
jet ski
Top
50
Spot!
jumper
5
juniper
25

juggling balls
jogger
jacuzzi
Top Spot!
Jack Russell
jigsaw
Jaguar
jellyfish

kaleidoscope
kayak
25
knife
5
killer whale
5
ketchup
Top
50
Spot!
kiwi fruit
10
10
kite

key
knitting
kale
koi carp
Top
Spot!
kettle
kingfisher
knot

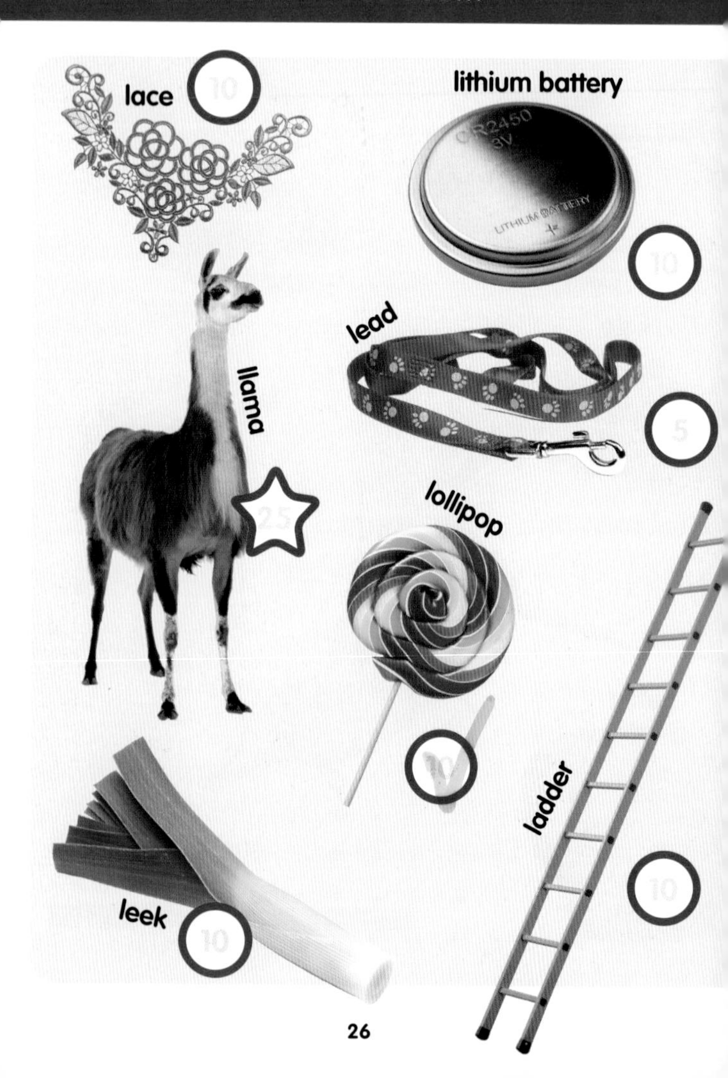
lace
10
lithium battery
CR2450
3V
LITHIUM BATTERY
10
lead
5
llama
25
lollipop
10
ladder
10
leek
10

Lego™
ladybird
lifeguard
LIFEGUARD
Labrador
lighthouse
Top
Spot!
log cabin
lamb
Top
Spot!

mangle
Top 40 Spot!
mango
15
mobile phone
mop
5
mirror
5
5
mackerel
15
mouth organ
20

m

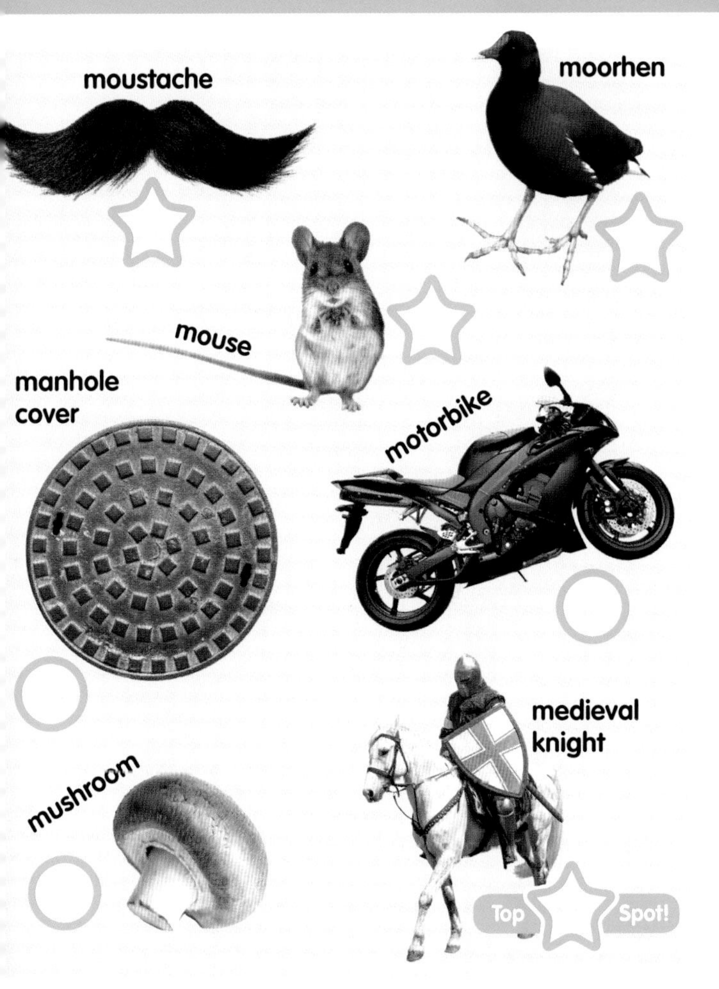
moustache
moorhen
mouse
manhole
cover
motorbike
medieval
knight
mushroom
Top
Spot!

noticeboard
10
10
no entry sign
nuthatch
15
nutmeg
Top
50
Spot!
necklace
nachos
10
10
5
needle

nurse
neon sign
nest
net
nettle
newt
Top Spot!
noodles

oak tree
20
owl
30
orchid
15
oats
10
oli
10
oboe
30
onion
5
omelette
10

octopus
oxygen tank
Top Spot!
oil painting
origami
oil rig
Top Spot!
okra

pizza
10
police
officer
20
postbox
pencil case
5
5
pine con
15
penny
farthing
Top
50
Spot!
plant pot
10

plate
playing cards
acock
portico
potato
Top
Spot!
prawn
poodle

quiz sheet
quince
25
20
queue
quarter past
12
11
1
10
2
9
3
8
4
7
6
5
quartz
25
quiche
quail egg

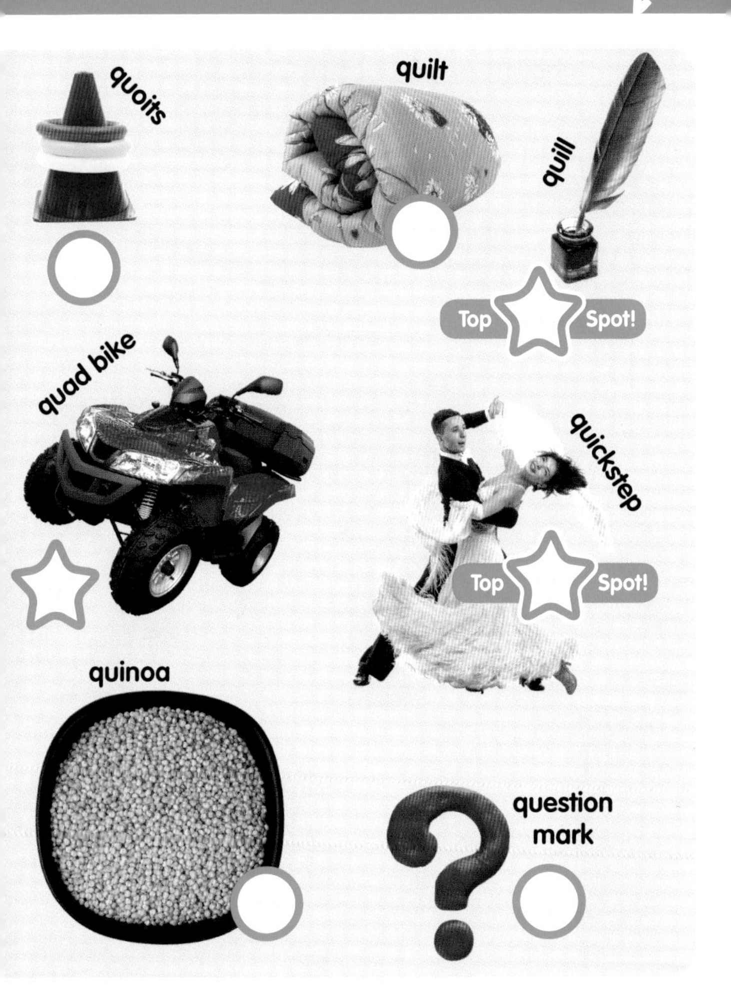
quoits
quilt
quill
Top Spot!
quad bike
quickstep
Top Spot!
quinoa
question
mark

rabbit
10
rhubarb
10
robin
10
recycling bin
5
rock climber
recorder
15
remote control
5
rose
10
Top 50 Spo

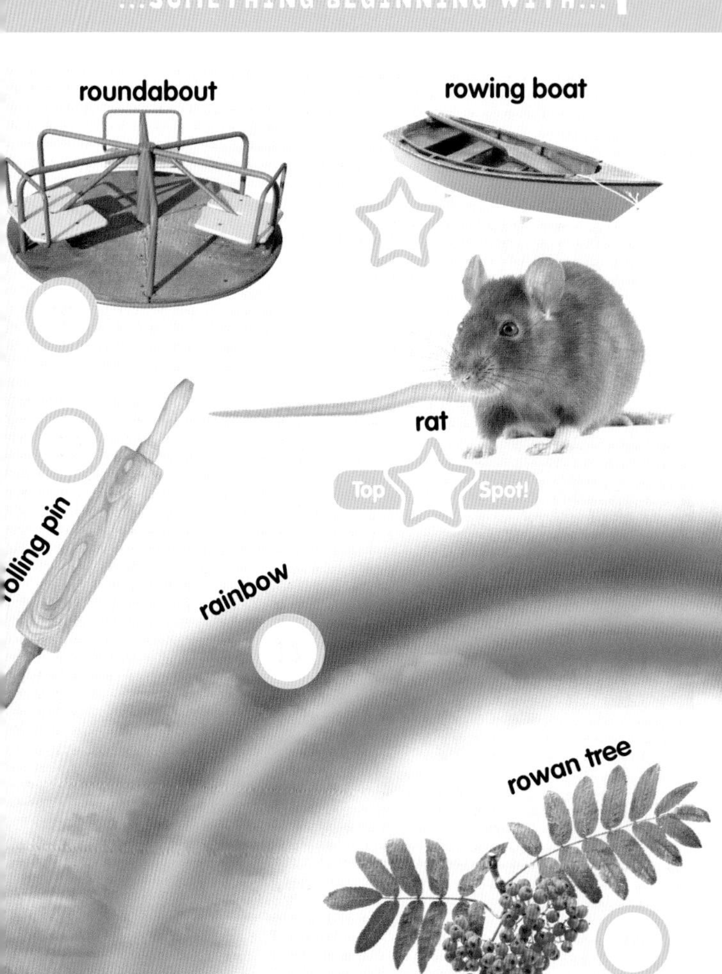
roundabout
rowing boat
rat
Top
Spot!
rolling pin
rainbow
rowan tree

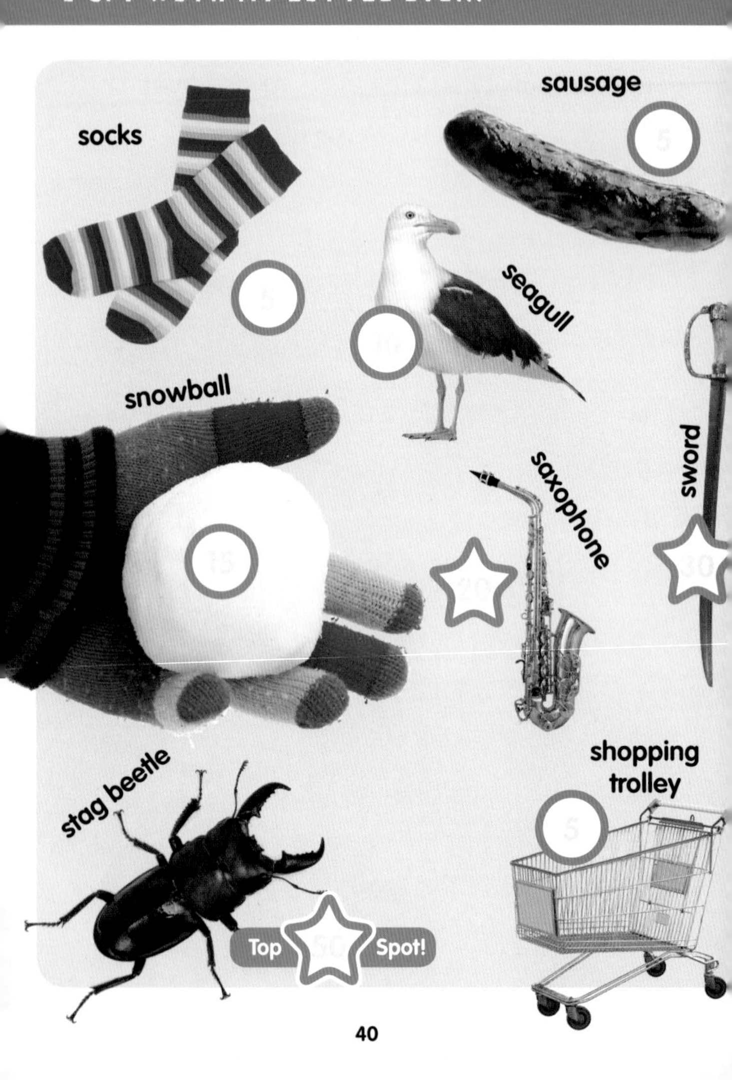
socks
sausage
seagull
snowball
sword
saxophone
shopping trolley
stag beetle
Top Spot!

skip
sleeping bag
snake
sundial
60103
nflower
steam train
Top
Spot!

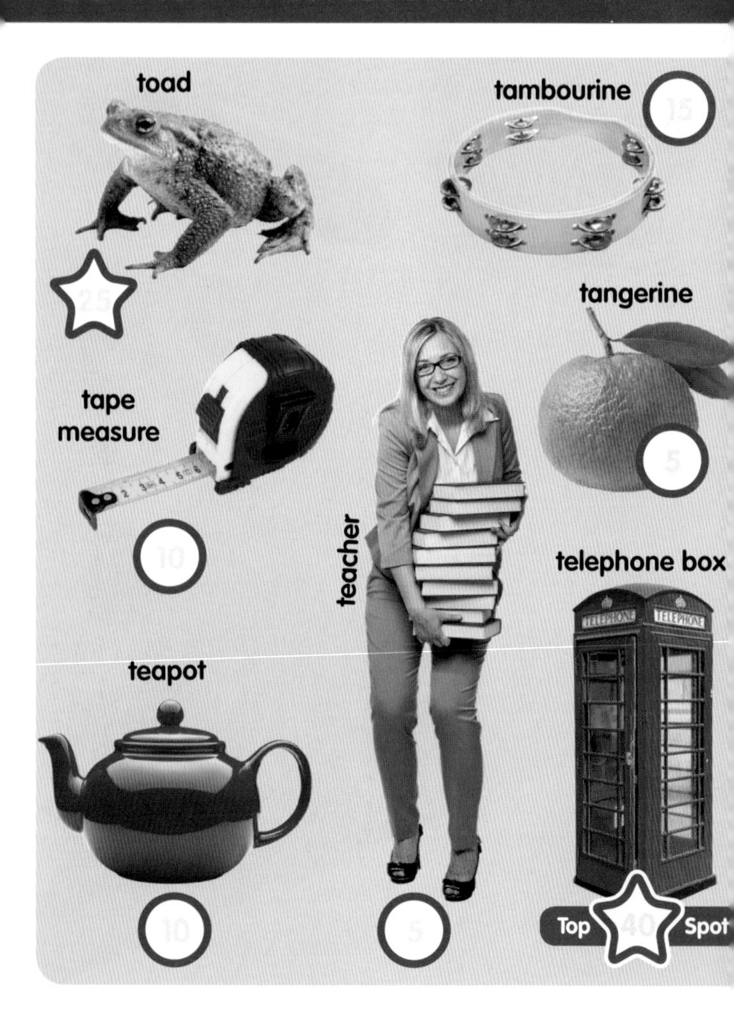
toad
25
tambourine
15
tangerine
5
tape
measure
10
teacher
5
telephone box
TELEPHONE
TELEPHONE
teapot
10
Top
40
Spot

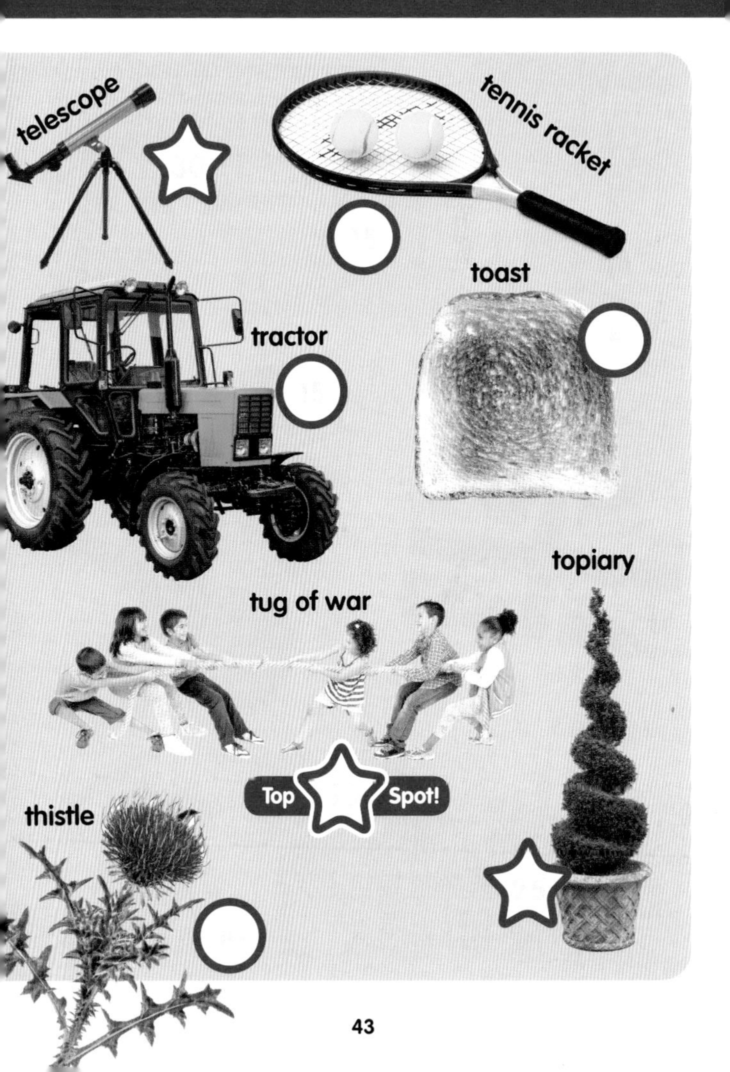
telescope
tennis racket
toast
tractor
topiary
tug of war
Top Spot!
thistle

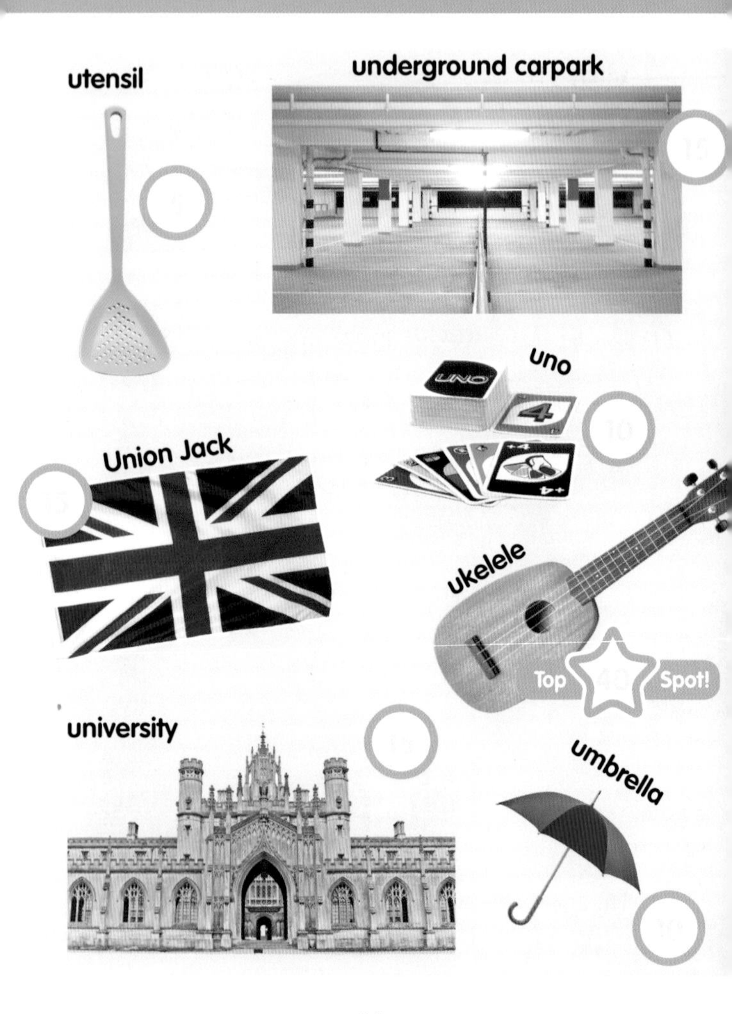
utensil
underground carpark
uno
UNO
Union Jack
ukelele
Top
Spot!
university
umbrella

utility vehicle
underpants
umpire
underground sign
UNDERGROUND
unicycle
uniform
upside-down cake
Top Spot!

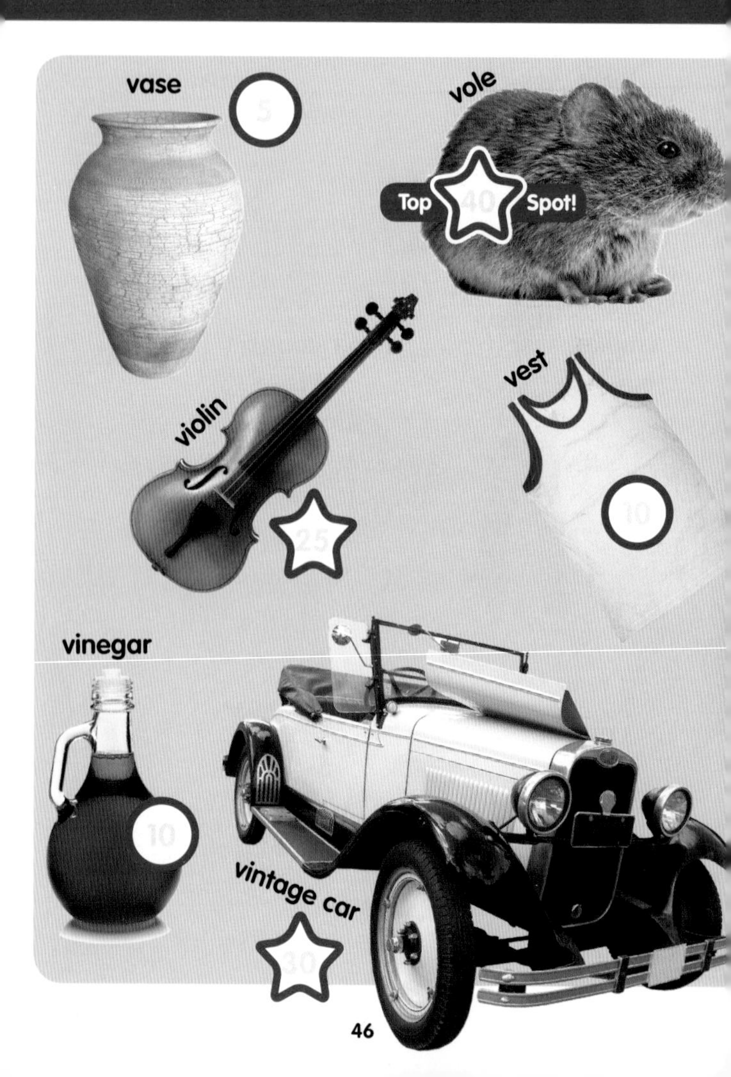
vase
5
vole
Top
40
Spot!
violin
25
vest
10
vinegar
10
vintage car
30

vegetables
velvet chair
violet
vanilla pod
van
Top Spot!
Velcro™
varnish
'ictoria Cross

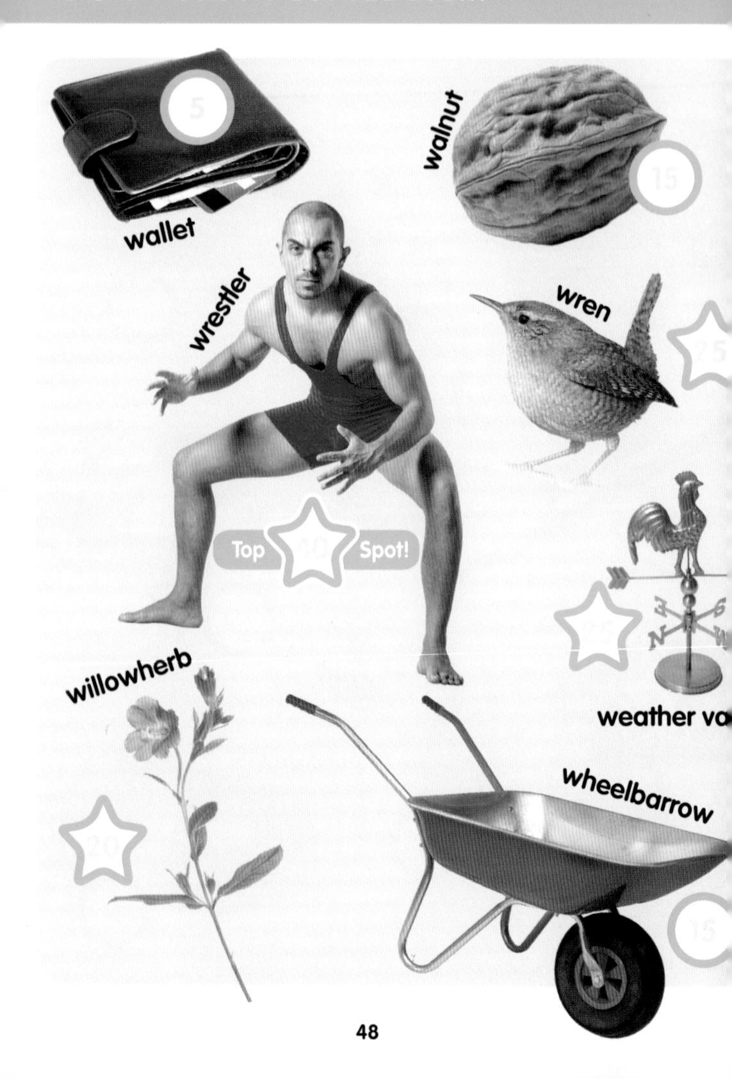
wallet
5
walnut
15
wrestler
wren
25
Top
10
Spot!
willowherb
weather va
wheelbarrow
20
15

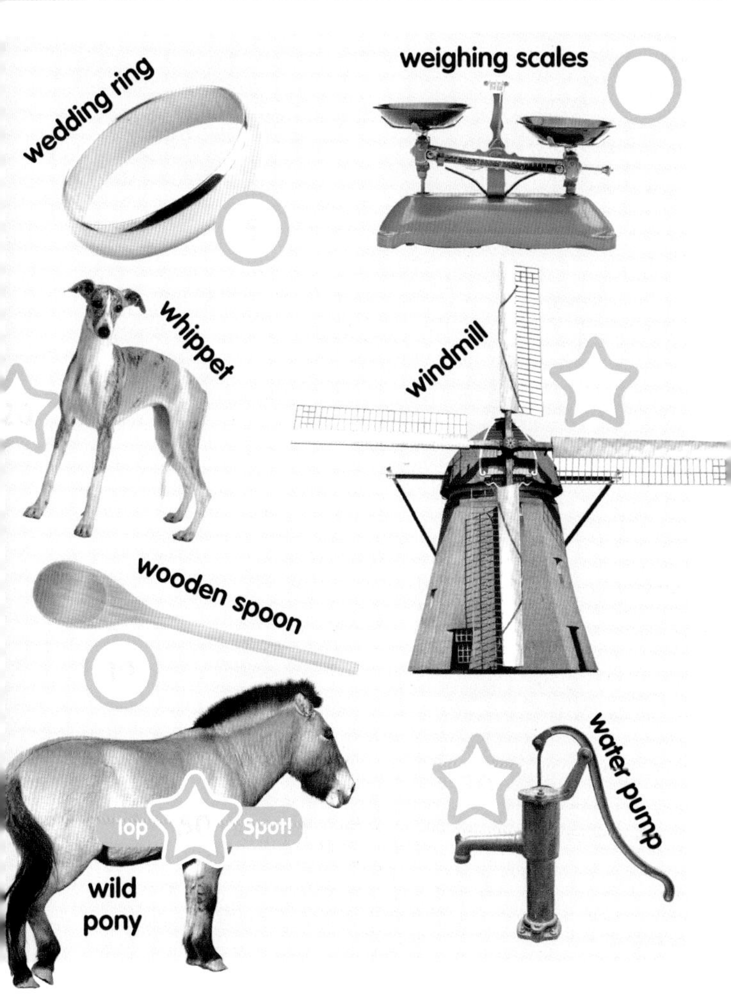

weighing scales
wedding ring
whippet
windmill
wooden spoon
water pump
lop
Spot!
wild pony

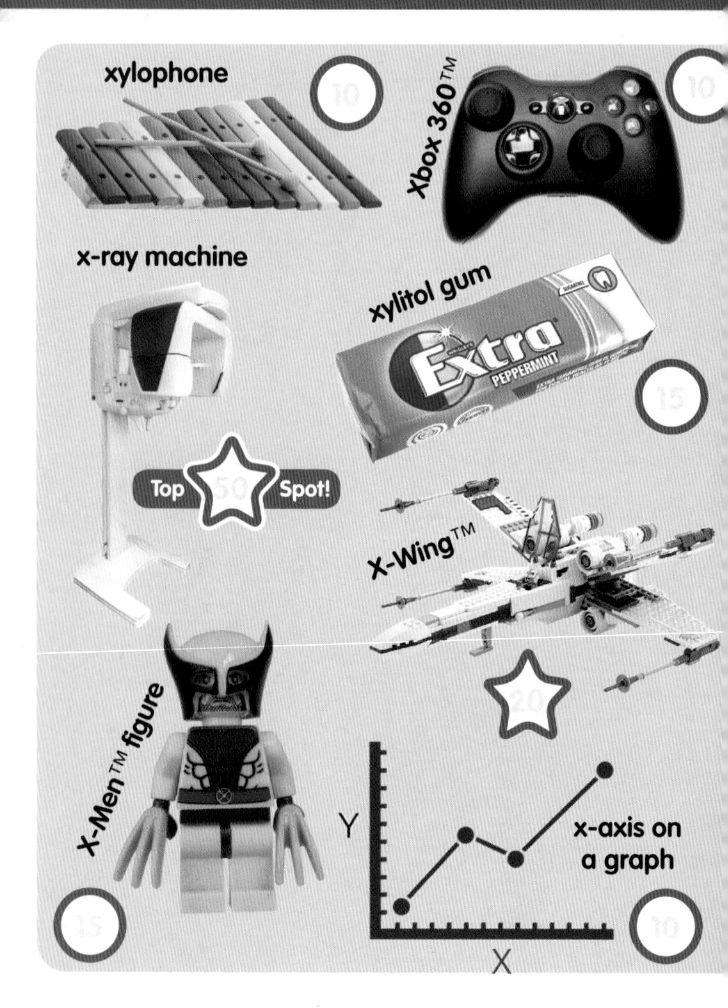
xylophone
10
Xbox 360™
10
x-ray machine
xylitol gum
Extra
PEPPERMINT
15
Top
50
Spot!
X-Wing™
20
X-Men™ figure
Y
x-axis on
a graph
X
15
10

xanthan gum
xenon bulb
Xmas tree
x marks the spot
xtreme sportsperson
xl size label
Size
XL
x roman numeral
X
Top
Spot!

yo-yo
10
yarn
yucca
yolk
10
10
20
yurt
yacht
25
Top
50
Spot!

yeast
yellow pages
Phone Book
yellowhammer
yoga pose
yoghurt
Top
Spot!
yew tree
Yorkshire
terrier

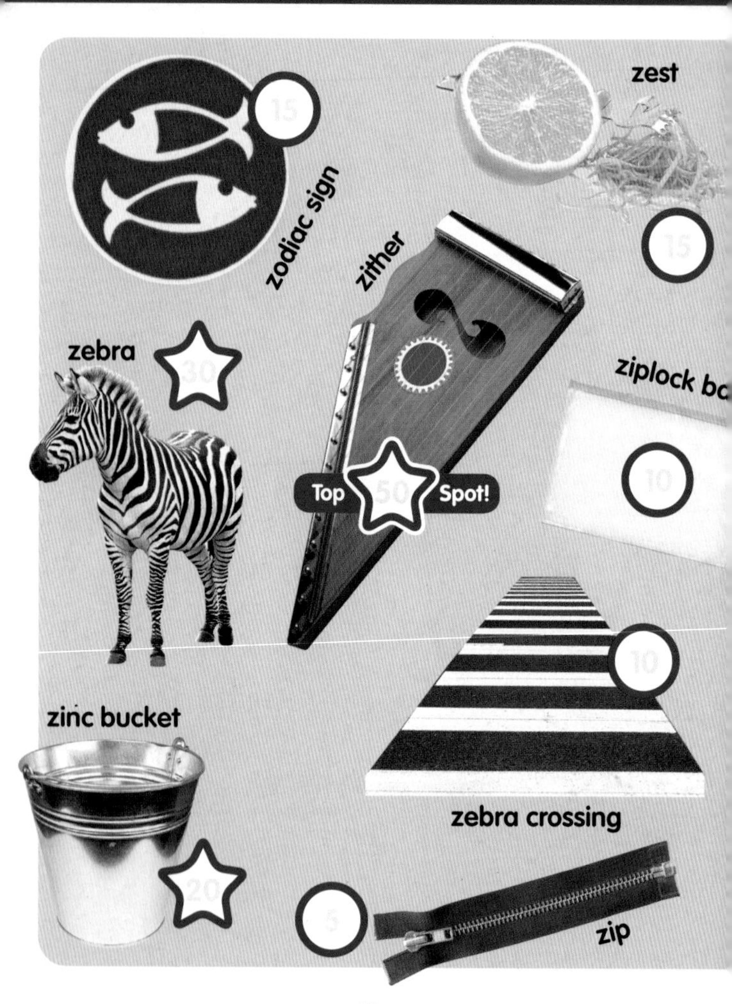
zest
15
zodiac sign
15
zither
zebra
30
ziplock ba
10
Top
50
Spot!
10
zinc bucket
zebra crossing
20
5
zip

zebra finch
Top Spot!
zigzag scissors
zoom lens
zookeeper
zone
20
ZONE

Throughout this book we have tried to give you a lot of ideas for things you can spot when you are out and about with your friends and family. There will always be new things to find however and these next few pages give you the chance to record some of the more interesting things you come across while playing i-SPY. You might even want to award yourself with a score – think 5–15 for easier spots, 20–30 for hard ones and 40 or 50 for Top Spots that should be almost impossible to find for all but the best spotters.

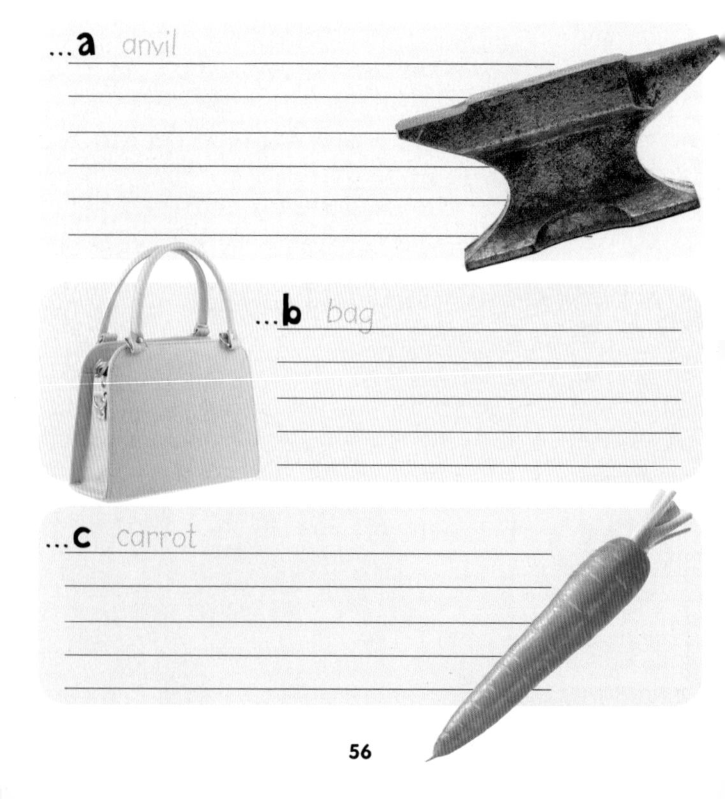

...d dentist
...e engagement ring
...f fig rolls
...g guitar
...h hiking boots

...i invitation

Wedding Invitation

...j jelly babies

...k kangaroo

...l library books

...m magnifying glass

...n nail polish

...o oil can

...p paintbrush

...q quesadillas

...r reindeer

...**s** sofa

...**t** tiger cub

...**u** unfinished painting

...V volleyball

...W washing machine

...X x key

...Y yellow rose

...Z zentangle drawing

INDEX

INDEX

i-SPY

How to get your i-SPY certificate and badge

Let us know when you've become a super-spotter with 1000 points and we'll send you a special certificate and badge!

HERE'S WHAT TO DO!

- Ask an adult to check your score.
- Visit www.collins.co.uk/i-SPY to apply for your certificate. If you are under the age of 13 you will need a parent or guardian to do this.
- We'll send your certificate via email and you'll receive a brilliant badge through the post!